Simple Canvas Work

Colour photographs by Robert Golden

Simple Canvas Work

Joan Nicholson

B T Batsford Limited

First published 1973

ISBN 0 7134 2480 X

Filmset by Keyspools Ltd, Golborne, Lancs
Printed and bound in Great Britain by
C Tinling & Co Ltd, Prescot and London
for the publishers
B T Batsford Limited
4 Fitzhardinge Street, London W1H 0AH

Contents

Introduction

Canvas work is a restful and absorbing form of embroidery. No expensive equipment or materials are needed, and there are no complicated techniques. All that is required is a few skeins of wool or cotton, a tapestry needle—which is a needle with a blunt point—and a piece of canvas. All are obtainable from a local store.

As in a painting, the bare canvas is gradually covered with a rich surface of colour and texture which can be transformed into a picture, a pincushion, a belt, or indeed into a fabric to be used as upholstery material, or for a waistcoat. A design can be chosen that will take months to complete, or a pleasant evening can be spent making a small but special present.

Half cross stitch is the only stitch used for all the designs in this book. It can be mastered in a matter of minutes. It has been chosen because of its versatility and the speed with which it can be worked. For the more experienced embroiderer and for those wishing to experiment, many different stitches can be used, and interesting results achieved.

Canvas work is an ideal craft for those who like to work at their own pace. The actual execution of the embroidery is relaxing and the use of a canvas marked out into a grid of squares helps to remove any intimidation the embroiderer may feel when first attempting a design.

Small spot patterns or repeats worked in and around the squares give exercises in the use of colour as well as practice in the use of needle and thread, and the establishment of an even tension. With practice the worker will be able to tackle with confidence and ease more ambitious designs using the scaffolding of the grid on which to build.

Both creating the design and working the embroidery give great enjoyment. Patterns can be worked out first on graph paper using crayons, felt-tip pens, or paints. Items can be designed to blend with and complement existing colour schemes in the home or for dress accessories.

Time and tedium are important factors to be taken into account when deciding what to make. It is better to tackle and finish a small piece of work than to attempt some ambitious project and have to admit defeat and leave it unfinished. There must be many homes in which hidden away in some drawer lurks a first attempt at craft work which has never been completed.

For a first attempt it is a good idea to make something that can be completed in an evening. In this way the initial enthusiasm is not diminished or, if the work does not quite come up to expectations, no harm is done and a new start can be made without any loss of face.

Pieces of canvas, about 100 mm or 125 mm (4 in. or 5 in.) square, can be made up into attractive items. Forming a patchwork they can be made into cushions or chair seats. Similarly, small strips make pencil cases, purses and hair bands. Such small pieces of canvas can easily be carried about in a pocket or handbag to be worked in odd leisure moments, or used to pass the time on a journey.

A 75 mm (3 in.) square of canvas embroidery worked either in wool or soft cotton can be made into a pincushion. Those illustrated on pages 36 and 37 were made from such squares backed with a scrap of velvet.

An attractive greetings card can be made by mounting a small piece of embroidery on a piece of card (see pages 32 and 34). A butterfly makes an easy subject for this, also a flower shape, or a decorative initial.

Three important factors lead to success.
1 The work should be within the capacity of the embroiderer.
2 It should be small enough to complete while the interest lasts.
3 It should be interesting enough in content and design to hold the attention of the embroiderer throughout.
If working an article is the slavish copying or filling in of a design it often becomes an exercise in endurance. It will never give the sense of achievement as does something made and designed by the embroiderer herself. Having to solve problems and make decisions gives an incentive to experiment. From then on any work done is a progression of ideas and can lead to real satisfaction.

It is useful to have several items of different kinds in preparation at the same time, for instance, a large piece of work on a frame, a set of squares to make into a cushion, and a belt or a bag. There is then always a choice of work to suit the embroiderer's mood or situation.

Embroiderers should be encouraged to experiment with different kinds of canvas mesh and to add new stitches to give a variety of textures. It is only by experimenting that the possibilities of the medium and the worker's own capabilities are discovered.

All the examples shown are experiments and are illustrated to give ideas. They are starting points from which to proceed, and it is hoped that they might suggest further ideas.

Equipment

Canvas

The items illustrated have been worked on a 25 mm (1 in.) squared canvas but any double thread canvas can be used successfully. If using the squared canvas, the red lines must always be vertical. This is important when making articles from units which are to be assembled, as the coloured woven threads act as a guide when sewing the pieces together and make it much easier.

All canvas is specially treated to produce the rigid surface necessary to hold the stitches in place and should not be crumpled or crushed. If it does become so accidentally, lightly press with a warm iron and a damp cloth (on the wrong side of any embroidery) to restore the crispness. Because the canvas is treated with a stiffening agent, embroidered items should be dry cleaned, not washed.

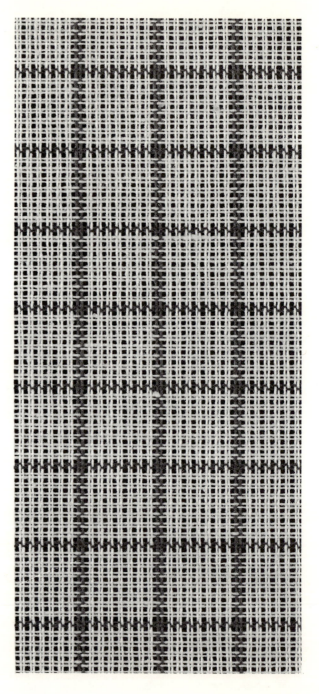

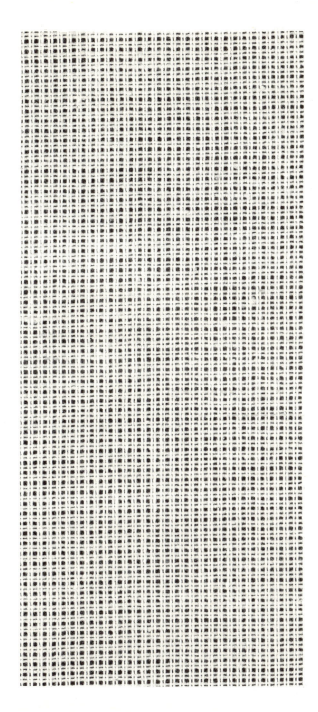

Needle

The needle used for canvas work has a large eye and a blunt point, two useful factors. The blunt point of the needle finds the spaces between the canvas mesh easily, and is pleasant to handle, working smoothly without pricking fingers or catching in the work. It is easily threaded by wrapping the end of a length of wool round the head of the needle, pinching it closely together between finger and thumb as it is slid up and off the needle, and then pushing the folded wool through the eye.

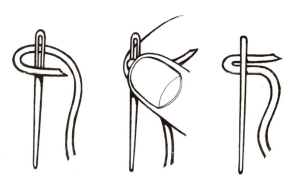

Scissors and tapestry needles

A small pair of **embroidery scissors** with fine points is useful for any necessary unpicking, and a packet of **tapestry needles** as it is helpful to have two or more needles threaded at the same time to try out different effects.

Linen thread

Strong linen thread is needed for joining the squares together.

Graph paper

For working out ideas for designs a new type of graph paper has been developed to correspond with the squared canvas. This is a valuable aid to design and many pattern variations can be worked out in detail first. It may be found helpful when using this paper, which is printed boldly, to mask off with plain paper the area around which one is working. Alternatively cut out a piece of graph paper of the size required for the design. Even a small scrap is useful to have handy when working, to solve design problems and thus often saves unpicking.

Ordinary graph paper can of course be used.

It is enjoyable to build up patterns and designs with crayons, felt-tip pens or paints prior to actually making them into embroideries. It is easy to begin with a simple repeated unit and gradually follow some of the more complex variations of colour, pattern and counterchange, examples of which are shown on page 44.

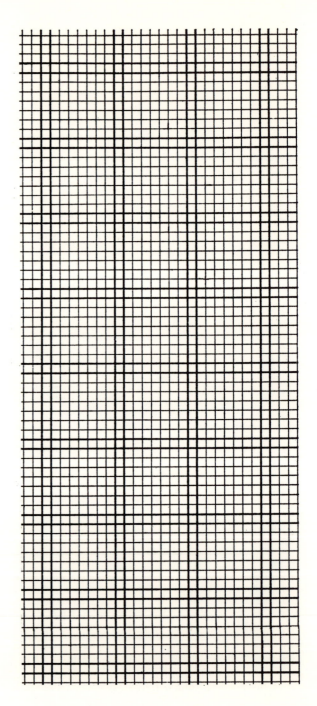

The stitch

Half cross stitch is worked in two movements, stabbing the needle up and down through the canvas, and working over the double threads as shown in the diagrams. This gives a diagonal stitch on the front and a short straight stitch at the back. This extremely easy stitch is all that is required, though a knowledge of other canvas stitches would help to vary the texture of work.

To ensure complete canvas coverage, short lengths of wool about 305 mm (12 in.) long should be used as the rough canvas tends to reduce the bulk of the wool if it is used for some time.

An even tension is quickly achieved after a little practice. The stitches should be kept fairly loose and 'fat'. When finishing off it should be easy to slip the needle through the back of the last few stitches to secure the wool, as shown in the diagram.

Never start with a knot. Either work over the end of the wool for the first few stitches, as shown, or begin by slipping the wool under the back of stitches already worked.

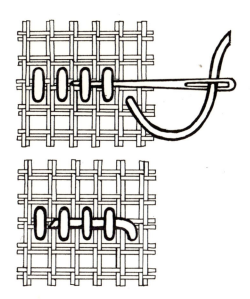

Embroidery frames

Most of the work illustrated in this book was done without a frame but any piece of canvas that cannot be handled and kept rigid during the working of the embroidery should be put into a frame to hold it flat. It is pleasant to work in this way with both hands free. Always work in a good light and have a comfortable chair at the right height when working with a frame.

Many different types of embroidery frames can be purchased. Some frames are made so that the work can be rolled up and carried about. Others make attractive items of furniture, especially when they contain a piece of embroidery being worked. Pin a piece of clear plastic sheet over the embroidery. This allows it to be seen and admired without the danger of it becoming soiled.

An old plain picture frame slightly larger than the piece of canvas to be worked can be used as a makeshift frame. Lash the canvas onto the frame all round to keep it taut.

Colour

We can express ourselves in many ways other than in words. Colour can be exciting or restful, patterns can move about in chaos or by their quiet repetition give a feeling of order and peace. Our reactions to these are often influenced by memories from early childhood and evoke emotions of a personal kind.

Experience of colour awareness grows quickly, likewise appreciation of the subtleties of varying tones of colour in their juxtaposition to others. A lively mixture of yellows and greens in profusion would conjure up for most people a feeling of life, of springtime perhaps. A chaos of black, red and purple would produce a dramatic sensation or a feeling of apprehension.

Because reaction to colour is a very personal thing, we develop tastes and sensitivities which grow in their subtlety. As in our tastes for literature or for food, we select and we become more critical as our knowledge increases. We begin to be able to imagine a design or a colour scheme to create the mood or the impression we want.

To be able to spill out a brightly coloured collection of threads from which to select is one of the happiest parts of working an embroidery. Although two colours or just black and white are enough to begin a design, it is of course helpful to build up gradually a good selection of colours.

To the fashion-conscious young, hectic colourings are exciting, unusual combinations of colour stimulating and evocative. But for the most part in choosing colour the function of the article to be made largely dictates the colours to be used.

Choosing colours and putting them together to obtain the desired effect can be a problem. Like most abilities it comes with experience. More is known of the intelligent and interesting use of colour today simply because there is so much around for us to see and from which to select in every sphere of living.

Always choose colours by daylight and see that there is sufficient of each colour to continue working with in the evening when using electric light, as it is easy to misjudge the shade of a colour by artificial light.

It is a great help when making decisions about colour to be able to place various ready mixed hues and tones together to see the effect, and this can be done so easily in embroidery. By actually handling the skeins of wool or cotton and trying out various combinations of colour and tone, one finds great enjoyment and the problem becomes a pleasure. We have today much more subtle shades and many tones of each colour, the tone of a colour being its depth or intensity. Two different hues, red and green perhaps, could be the same tone. If a black and white photograph were taken of them they would appear the same. By carefully studying the disposition of the light, dark and medium tonal values of colours used, which are as much part of the design as the actual shapes and lines, it can be decided how to give vitality to the designs.

Different colours and tonal values can alter a design completely. A design worked in black and white looks most spectacular when the areas worked in each are large. If the areas worked in the black and white threads are split up into very small shapes the effect will be of greyness. So a design worked in two shades of one colour would look more subdued the closer these two shades are to each other. The greater the difference in the tonal values of the colour the bolder the effect.

A gem-like eye-catcher of a cushion may be envisaged for a white or a dark room; a sombre rich patterned panel for a smooth white wall. Texture and colour are at the command of the worker in needlecraft of this kind, also richness of pattern and brilliance of colour, but they must be used with discretion to produce effective results. Many tones of the same colour always produce a more intense effect than all the colours of the spectrum put together.

For anyone who develops a keen interest in the craft, or for teachers in schools, a varied palette of coloured wools should be gradually acquired and kept available. Put together in related groups, the yellows, greens and blues, the pinks, reds and purples, they form a palette of colours from which selections can be made of shades that blend and complement, excite or soothe. A chance grouping of a few strands of wool often gives a lead to a new and unusual colour scheme.

There is sometimes a problem of where to store the increasing volume of skeins. A large transparent plastic bag is useful and inexpensive. The skeins are kept clean and are easily carried from place to place. They can be seen at a glance and it is easy to select a particular shade from anywhere in the bag when working without emptying them all out.

It is very important never to store the canvas and wool together. They must be kept separately as the rough edges of the canvas tease out the wool.

Occasionally the bag of skeins of wool needs to be sorted, and when doing this it is useful to keep a few elastic bands handy and when it is noticed how attractive certain accidental groupings of colours look, slip a band around these skeins, or deliberately try to find unusual and exciting mixtures of colours and keep these together. When beginning a new piece of work these colours may suggest an idea.

Decide what new colours are needed to enrich the palette, or plan an embroidery using colours found pleasing in a fabric or carpet design or a wallpaper and try to purchase similar colours.

For small pieces of work, for example the patchwork pieces for cushions, small baskets of the sort used for bread rolls are suitable for keeping the materials which are being worked together, but again it is always advisable to put the canvas squares into a small plastic bag or an envelope and not keep them mixed up with the skeins of wool.

There will be times when it is only possible to work for short periods; sometimes there will be many distractions. Leave important decisions about colour and design to a time when complete attention can be given to the work; this saves a good deal of unpicking. At other times it is possible to carry on a conversation or even watch television while working over parts of a design that have been decided.

Geometric designs

15

The materials needed for canvas embroidery are ▶
few. A handful of skeins of wool or cotton, a
tapestry needle and a piece of canvas. Start right
away with a needleful of thread, using graph
paper and a felt-tip pen to solve any details of
designing as work proceeds

Carpet design
for Wilton
*Reproduced by
courtesy of the
Design Council*

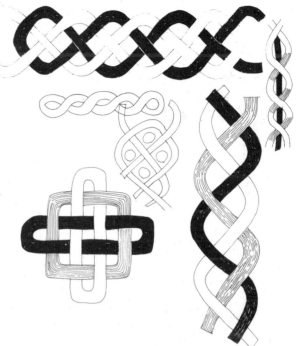

Overleaf

Inventing patterns can be as absorbing as doing crossword puzzles and a source of great pleasure and relaxation. The two tartan patterns, top right, were found among many experimental patterns on a sampler in the Victoria and Albert Museum worked more than 100 years ago. These would look very attractive in a room today worked over a chair seat or stool top. With the wonderful palette of coloured wools now available designs do not need to be elaborate to be effective. Simple repeats in well chosen colours can make delightful and novel upholstery fabrics

Experiment with the use of colour. Imagine the effect of one colour overlapping another. Make a sampler using many shades of one colour, or several different colours meeting each other in discord and harmony, and use the ideas produced in future designs

Belts

A length of canvas about 205 mm (8 in.) longer than the waist measurement is needed for a belt that fastens with a buckle. For a belt that has a clasp or that laces up, the piece of canvas should be about the same size as the waist (or the hip measurement, if the belt is to be worn low). In both cases allow 25 mm (1 in.) extra all round the embroidered area.

Roll the strip of canvas and work the embroidery as shown. If preferred the belt can be worked in two pieces, cutting the strip in half and joining them together later. When the embroidery is completed, press on the wrong side using a damp cloth. Trim away the canvas to within five double threads (five stitch spaces) of the embroidery. Cut a piece of lining material the length and width of the canvas. Do not choose a slippery fabric as this would be difficult to handle. Tack the lining to the belt along one long edge only, right sides together. With the reverse side of the embroidery uppermost, machine or hand stitch the two pieces together. Take the stitches actually into the last holes used for the embroidery all the way to make a neat seam, and ensure that no canvas threads show. Turn the lining over the back of the work and tack the seam down along the other long side of the canvas, trimming the corners a little to make a neat seam. Turn in and tack the corresponding edges of the lining, allowing it to come slightly over the canvas edge.

Tack and then slip stitch the two edges together, rolling the edge of the lining slightly over the canvas edge. Sew the ends firmly and neatly, making a point at one end if a buckle is used. Press, using a warm iron and damp cloth.

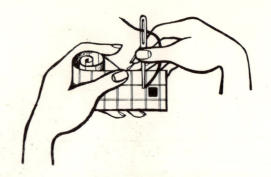

Eyelet holes can be made with a special inexpensive tool when the embroidery is finished and lined, and this also helps to give a professional touch. The punching and making of eyelet holes allows leather thonging to be used whether as an added decoration or for lace-up fastenings.

Hair bands

For a band for the hair, follow the same method, making the band either to go all round the head, Indian fashion, in which case allow for a seam, or a strip 305 mm to 380 mm (12 in. to 15 in.) would make a band which ties under the hair. In this case make ties of the lining material or attach elastic covered with a tube of the lining allowing for stretch.

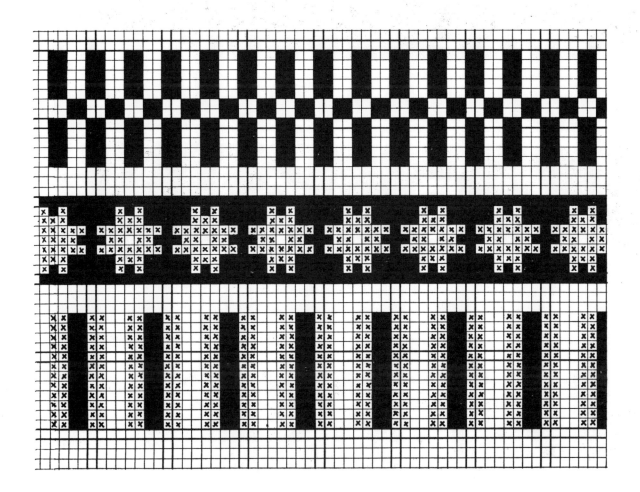

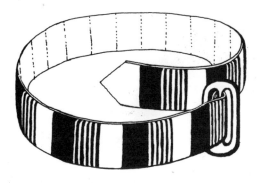

Overleaf

It is sometimes easier to work out ideas directly on to the canvas. These samplers can then be used as reference when patterns are needed. Strip patterns like these would make curtain bands, pelmets, or bellpulls

A belt can be made quite easily and in colours to complement an outfit. Line it with a scrap of bright material, and use an eyelet tool to give a professional finish

23

Fur patterns

Nature's protective camouflage patterns are interesting, from the jazzy stripes of zebras to the delicate tracery on butterflies' wings. The bold and often bizarre markings and dramatic colourings of animal furs have given to every fashion era from the Stone Age onwards a fillip that no man-made fabric can rival.

A fur effect embroidery can be fun to do. It could make a glamorous dress accessory, or a decorative addition to a room without giving rise to any qualms of conscience.

No drawing is necessary though some preliminary sketches or doodles may be helpful. Have a really good look at the next tabby cat that goes by. Visit the natural history department of the local museum. Books from the library with photographs of big game animals, especially of tigers, which are beautifully marked might give further ideas.

Work outwards from a centre line which would be made easier using the squared canvas. Make the contours flow in bold splashings of black, white and tawny colours. Let the lines move over the surface freely to completely fill the shape you are designing for.

Once interest has been aroused in producing these fur patterns, they will be found enjoyable to do and can be used for many purposes. It will help the embroiderer to appreciate the intricacies involved in breaking down a shape by cutting it up with bold slashes and stripes of dark and light. Such fur patterns would make belts which would add an original and dramatic effect to any costume, and could be worn with trousers or a dress. The contrast of the bold design with a shiny brass buckle and a vivid lining would give the embroidery the right presentation. Remember that a belt will flatter the waist if there are more vertical lines than horizontal ones.

Cushions and chair seats made with patterns of of this kind would lend an air of splendour to a room, perhaps even a large design of a complete tiger-skin pattern could be worked by an enthusiast as a mural, or a beginner might prefer to make waistcoat fronts, a hat or hatband, or an eye-catching shoulder bag.

Overleaf

Flags, banners and bunting give gay inspiration to the designer. The bold colouring and symmetrical shapes translate easily onto the canvas. Here is a Union Jack cushion worked as sixteen little separate flags then sewn together. The Valentine embroidery worked in wool with the addition of glass beads is reminiscent of the mementos worked by sailors a century or so ago

A fur effect embroidery can be fun to do and to wear. Fur patterns would make belts, hat bands, waistcoats or bags to add an original and dramatic effect to any outfit. Use a shining brass buckle and a vivid lining to give the embroidery its full impact

A piece of canvas worked in such a way combines well with knitting, or with jersey wool fabric and materials such as corduroy velvet, tartan and the rougher kinds of tweeds.

The addition of woollen fringes, braids or tassels to bags, belts and purses adds to their attractiveness and gives the finishing touch.

27

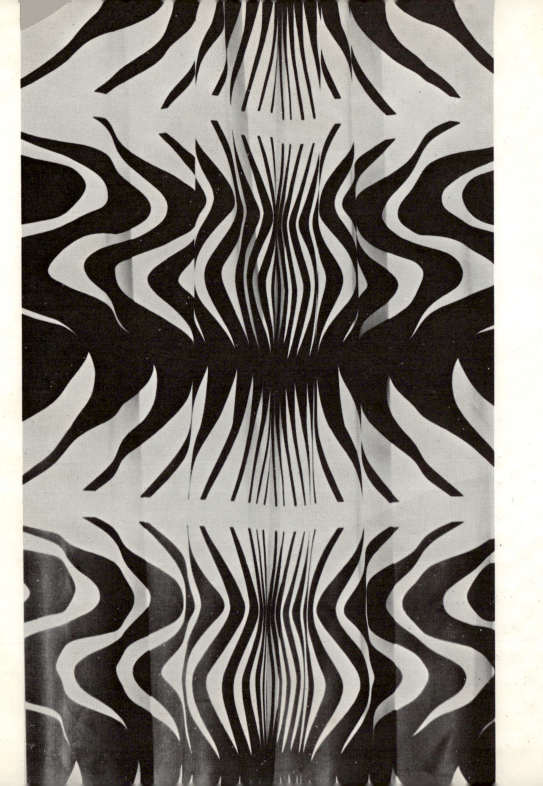

◄ Printed satin cotton designed
by Barbara Brown for
Heal Fabrics Limited

Overleaf
Many original and beautiful gifts can be made
from small pieces of embroidery. One small
square of embroidery mounted attractively makes
a very special greeting card that could be worked
in an evening. A belt, a box, a picture mount or a
purse would make treasured Christmas or birthday presents for relatives or friends who appreciate
something personal and unique

Figures in costume afford endless inspiration and
give much scope for the inventive use of colour
and pattern making. Taking a centre line the
design can be quickly built up using graph paper
or the squared canvas. Symmetrical designs such
as these are easy to make with some reference
from a library for historical details. A series of
pictures of figures in costume would make a
feature in a room and provide a pleasant occupation

GREETINGS

Greetings cards

A small piece of embroidery mounted in a card
which has been cut away to show the design
makes an original greetings card for a special
occasion or for a particular person who would
appreciate the fact that someone had worked it
for them. A butterfly was used in the example
shown overleaf, and this unit repeated could also
be made into a cushion. Flower shapes or even
geometric designs look well shown off in this
way, and need only take an hour or two to work.

Frames to pictures

As an alternative to presenting the embroidery
mounted in a card, a border of canvas work can be
used to surround a photograph or picture,
making it look more attractive and important.
There are many reproductions that could be
presented in this way. Even a postcard can be made
into something ornate that would add charm to a
room.

Borders can be of simple lines in colours to blend
with or flatter the picture itself or can be more
elaborate in the form of plaits or pleated and
twisting ribbons, repeating patterns, or geometrical shapes or flowers. These can be worked
out on graph paper first to solve the problem of
turning the corners satisfactorily. Only one corner

34

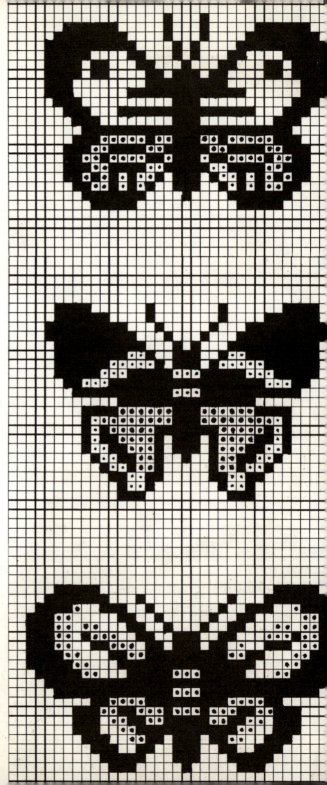

need to be plotted on the graph paper which can be turned to represent each corner as the work is carried out, the length of the sides being made to fit the picture. The same design can then be used to fit any picture by extending the repeat to the length needed. This means that several pictures can be made up into a set perhaps forming a decorative feature over one wall of a room.

When the embroidery is completed and pressed, trim away the canvas to within five stitch spaces of the work, turn in all the edges bending the canvas over on the first line of double threads just outside the embroidery and tack, mitreing the corners carefully. Be careful not to cut too near the embroidery especially on the inner edges. A little gum painted over the threads will prevent them from fraying or they can be carefully overstitched. The mount can be placed over the picture and the whole thing put in a frame with glass to protect it, or it can be presented with just the embroidered mount, using glass to protect the picture only if desired. In this case, cut a piece of card to the same size as the mount and cover it with felt, velvet, or some appropriate material using a rubber adhesive to stick it to the card.

A narrow piping can be applied to the mount on both the outside and inside edges to finish it off. This could be in a matching or contrasting colour or, to give a rich effect, gold or silver.

Using a fine metal crochet hook, a decorative edge can be worked into the canvas edge with metallic or any other interesting thread, taking one stitch into each hole in the canvas all round, using a double crochet stitch with perhaps a picot edge worked on top. Pin the mount to the backing and stitch them together or use adhesive. One side can be left open so that the picture can be changed.

Interlacing bands would also make borders of embroidered trim for dresses, suits or jackets.

Overleaf
Start with simple pattern making. Small spot patterns or repeats worked in and around the squares give exercises in the use of colour and practice in the use of needle and thread. These experimental pieces of embroidery can be used to make pin cushions or purses

Pincushions can be made in many different ways and make enjoyable practice pieces for someone learning to design and embroider, as well as providing attractive gifts for friends for Christmas or birthdays

Pincushions

To make a pincushion out of a square of embroidery similar to the ones illustrated use a piece of canvas leaving about 25 mm (1 in.) extra all the way round. When the embroidery is completed press the work using a damp cloth. Trim the canvas to within five double threads of the embroidery.

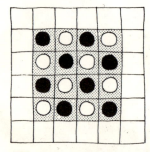 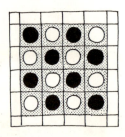

Cut a piece of backing material to this size—velvet, corduroy or heavy cotton weave would be suitable. Carefully pin and then tack the two pieces, right sides together.

Machine or hand stitch the side and bottom edges together, taking the stitches into the last holes used for the embroidery so that no canvas threads show and an absolutely straight line is made. Trim the corners. Carefully turn right side out.

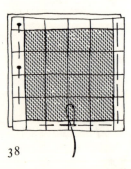 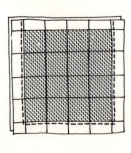

Stuff the pincushion fairly compactly with kapok, shredded nylon stocking or similar soft material. Fold in the top edges and slip stitch in place, drawing the pieces closely together.
Fasten off securely.

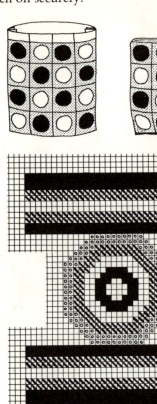

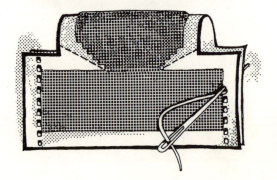

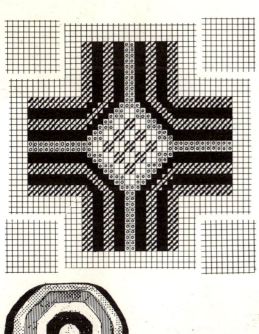

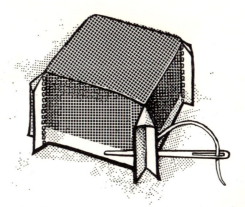

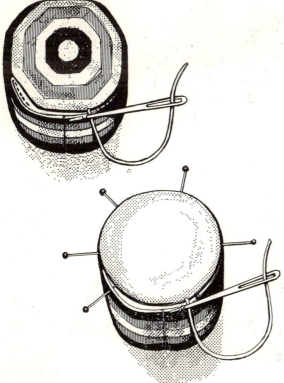

With a little more time pincushions of different shapes can be made such as the circular and cube shaped ones shown. These can be planned on graph paper first, letting the design emphasise the three-dimensional shapes.

Coloured glass headed pins make a decorative finish.

Overleaf

Making a cushion from small squares of canvas work could be a family occupation for holidays or winter evenings. Although one simple stitch only is used and the designs are entirely made up of triangles, the result can be brilliant and exciting if the colours used are cleverly chosen. Each simple design is repeated sixteen times forming a mosaic-like pattern when assembled. By adding more squares the cushion can be made larger

This design of a labyrinth taken from an old Cretan coin was worked boldly in red and black wool by a schoolgirl. It would look equally well in closely related colours or make a basic design for a set of cushions or chair seats all worked in different colours

Cushions

A cushion made up of units can be any size. Those illustrated on page 40 were made from sixteen units.

To assemble units

When all the squares have been worked press them lightly on the wrong side using a damp cloth, and ease them into shape. Trim away the surplus canvas to no less than five double threads, five stitch spaces, away from the embroidery. Make sure that the stitches all follow the same direction and that the patterns match.

Crease the canvas along the row of double threads just outside the embroidered area, folding it to the back. Fold over the corresponding side of the adjacent square. With right sides together line up the coloured thread bringing the double threads into perfect alignment.

Using a strong linen thread, and commencing with a knot, join the two pieces with a stab stitch as shown, taking the needle up and down between each pair of double threads of both pieces of canvas. Pass the needle under the creased edge only so that the stitching line is just above the embroidery as shown. Finish off by taking the needle back two or three stitches to secure the thread. This seam will draw the embroidered pieces close together and not allow any canvas threads to show on the front of the work.

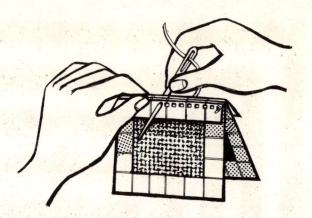

Continue joining the squares until four strips have been made. These are then creased and joined in the same way, matching the mesh as before. Take a back stitch at each intersection as shown. Press the assembled squares on the wrong side, flattening the ends of the seams on the canvas edge all round with the tip of the iron.

The back for a cushion of this type must be strong. Corduroy velvet was used for the ones shown. This makes a pleasing contrast to the embroidery. Cut a piece of backing material to the correct size and lay the embroidery on it right sides together. Pin and carefully tack in place. Machine stitch round leaving a gap on one side. Take the stitching line through the last holes used for the embroidery so that no canvas threads show. Trim the corners and turn right side out.

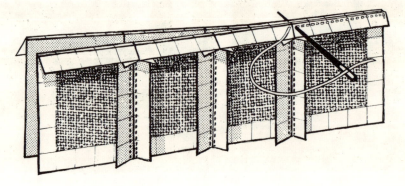

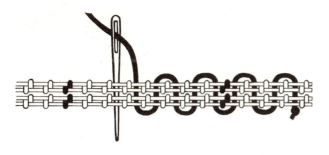

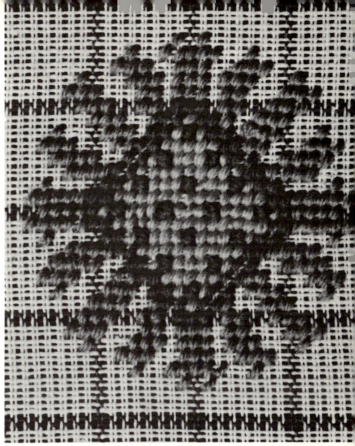

Make a cushion pad slightly larger than the size of the cover and insert. Close the gap with a slip stitch and press lightly again if necessary.

The same design on a square can be put together in different ways to alter the effect, and one design can be worked in several different colours to make a related set of cushions. These would make a colourful addition to a long couch or divan, or would make a set for dining chairs.

By rolling a strip of canvas so that it can be held in the hand (see page 22), a long piece can easily be worked. Such strips could also be made and assembled as described to form cushions. Large strips would make curtain bands and pelments which could transform the décor of a room.

A lining made from matching or contrasting cotton poplin is necessary for all of these items, and for furnishing trimmings, braids and cords add greatly to the finished effect.

Overleaf
Counterchange. This flower pattern is made lively by changing the background colour in each alternate square. One single pattern makes an attractive birthday or greetings card

Flowers have always been a popular source of design for embroidery. These pieces were worked using Anchor Soft Embroidery Cotton. The free use of simple shapes and colours for the band in the centre to suggest flowers and leaves contrasts with the formal patterns made by adapting natural forms and colours to the medium using squared canvas as a guide

43

All of these cushions were made from small units sewn together. The windmill pattern on the left has four small patterns on each square, the same design above has one pattern on each square worked in alternating colours making a bolder statement. Enlarging a design is made easy with the use of squared canvas

The design can be worked over a large area or
could be used for a strip of embroidery to make
a belt or trimming band

Boxes

Boxes made of canvas embroidery are interesting design problems. They should be made on the double box principle. Cover a thin cardboard duplicate of the embroidered shapes with lining material and insert this into the finished box, then sew the two pieces together. The same procedure is used to make the lid which should be slightly larger than the box.

Small glass beads can be used to great effect to decorate any of these items, taking a bead onto the needle (which must be a fine one) as the stitch is made and using waxed sewing thread:

◀ An embroidered design intended for a box and lid makes an interesting flat pattern too as the lines follow the contours of the shape for which it is intended

49

Designs for pincushions or cushions

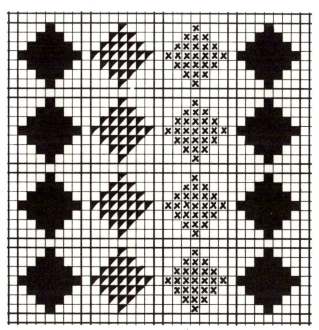

51

 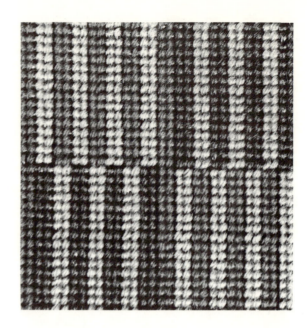

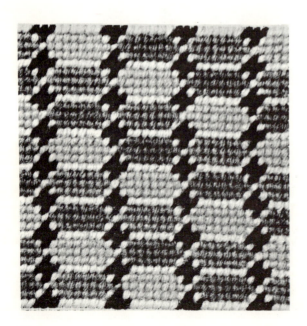 

Carpet designed for Wilton by W. Buchanan
Reproduced by courtesy of the Design Council

Designs from flowers

So many aspects of flowers and growing things have an appeal which can give inspiration to the designer of embroideries. The pattern of leaf, stem, and petal, the perfect packaging of seed in pod and leaf in bud provide endless ideas for those who spare the time to look and learn.

Herbals were often used as sources for plant designs for embroidery and the rather stiff decorative versions of plants which we still grow in our gardens today, such as carnations, honeysuckle and violets, were copied from woodcuts even to the extent of using the black outline and then filling in with colour.

Colour is one of the immediate attractions of flowers. The effect of blooms massed together in beds and borders, or filling a vase, can be conveyed by simple flower shapes worked in brilliant colours.

In the design on page 45 circles of various sizes have been used almost filling the whole area, sometimes overlapping. The remaining areas of canvas have then been filled in with shades of greens and greys to suggest foliage and shadow. No attempt has been made to show the flower heads in any detail or even to indicate what sort of flowers they are, but the general effect is one of richness of colour and an *impression* of masses of flowers. Such impressionistic designs can be most evocative, often capturing the effect more than naturalistically drawn individual flowers could.

By choosing colours which suggest certain varieties of blooms—petunias in shades of mauve and pink and white, michaelmas daisies in all shades of purple and blue, spring flowers, white, yellow and gold—the real and remembered effects of flowers can be captured.

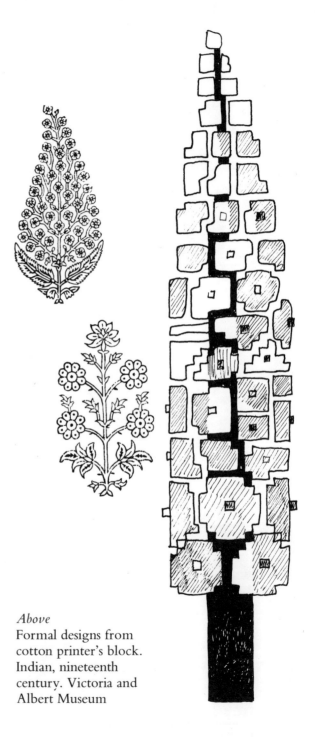

Above
Formal designs from cotton printer's block. Indian, nineteenth century. Victoria and Albert Museum

54

Embroidery for centuries endeavoured to copy paintings and tapestries. We are all familiar with the wool work cushions and chair seats of the last century where naturalistic flowers and fruit are presented and are so real it is almost uncomfortable to sit down there.

An effective way of producing flower designs which can be easily translated into canvas work is to find photographs of flowers of the sort shown in colour in bulb and gardening catalogues. These often have pictures of roses in bloom and many different varieties of popular flowers grown in gardens today.

Use tracing paper or thin detail paper and lightly draw around flowers and leaves. Arrange and build up a design moving the paper about. Draw in the basic shape of the flowers and leaves in a stencil-like way as though making a flower arrangement, suggesting the forms of petals and leaves only, using a light pencil line.

If a square or circular shape is required, half the design can be planned and then reversed to fill the shape by folding the paper and drawing the corresponding half in reverse.

When the composition has been assembled, slip a piece of graph paper (ten squares to 25 mm (1 in.)) under the tracing, and carefully re-draw the design more boldly, following the squares seen through from underneath which represent stitches, so translating the free drawing to a working drawing. This method can also be used for converting any freehand drawing to the discipline of working it to the threads of the canvas. The drawing can be coloured or tinted to suggest the disposition of light and dark shades, or work can begin straight away on the canvas choosing colours as you go and making alterations and improvements as the design takes shape.

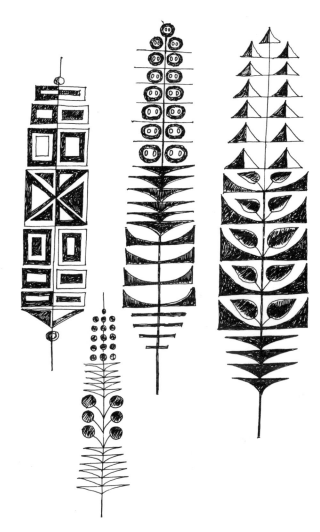

The degree of representation should be according to the embroiderer's requirement and experience, but even a simple two colour or three colour interpretation of flower inspired shapes and colours worked in this way can be most attractive and produce a lively disposition of lines and forms that otherwise might not have occurred. The sketch need only act as a guide and the design can be altered and improved as it is worked. This is one of the real pleasures of working a personal design. It is a really creative activity and an interest that continues until the work is completed. Decisions about colours become an absorbing part of the work, and are not diminished to the tedious copying of someone else's choice.

Botany books showing the floral formulae and structure of plants are valuable. These drawings used by the botanist to explain the make up of the various parts of a plant are easily translated into designs since the reduction of the complication of the plant growing in the wild to a line drawing is a great asset. Sections of flowers showing the structure with perhaps the seed pods and cross sections showing the symmetrical arrangement of the petals and sepals are very beautiful as patterns of lines and shapes.

When using plants for canvas designs it is important to omit any unecessary complications of form, and use only what is interesting and desirable in the growth habit or colour of the subject, or what appeals particularly to the designer. The finer the canvas the nearer the realism can be but on a mesh of ten stitches to 25 mm (1 in.) only certain aspects can be conveyed.

If a plant has six petals and this is not easy to manipulate on the canvas it is better to adapt the plant using a four or eight petal structure. One may copy an intricate natural form for a botanical reference or as a study, but in this context we are primarily looking for material for attractive embroidery design.

56

Colour can be used freely, but all structural forms and designs are dominated to a certain extent by the warp and weft over which they are worked. This does not necessarily mean limitation but rather adaptation of what is used, and this appreciation makes for good work.

Printed cotton furnishing fabric designed by Marcella Tanzi for *Heal Fabrics Limited* ▶

Ideas based on
the same principle

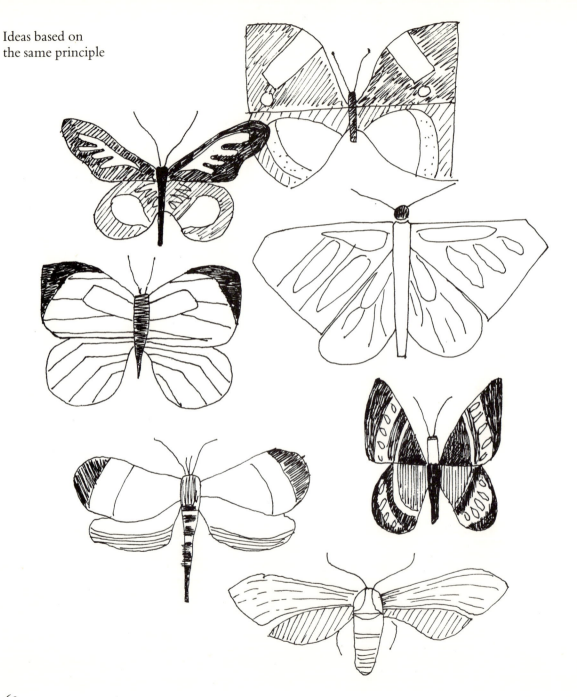

By making simple tracings over photographs of ▶
flowers and leaves new ideas for floral compositions and designs can be discovered. The patterns of light and shade between petals and leaves and branches giving a useful aid to the designer in filling areas with a balanced tonal effect

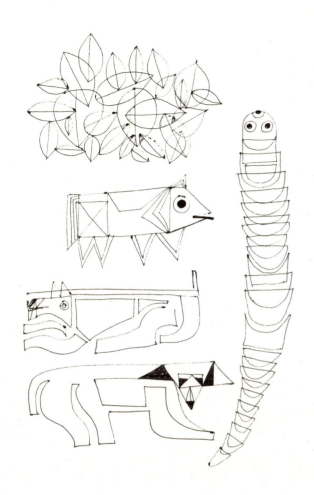

Overleaf
Large pieces of embroidery must be worked in a frame. This design intended for a stool top was suggested by a wallpaper pattern. Framed it could be used to liven a plain wall or serve as a firescreen. The cushion is worked in the bold primary colours and black found in a stained glass window. The use of one simple shape repeated in the various colours gives it the appearance of a piece of bright patchwork

An embroidered chess or draughts board. An unusual application of embroidery which is decorative and useful and makes an easy exercise in designing for a beginner. This one is framed in a simple wooden moulding, the surface protected by glass. It can be hung on the wall when not in use, or used as a tray

Purses or pencil cases with zip fastenings

When the embroidery has been completed, trim the canvas all round to within five stitch spaces of the embroidery. Press with embroidery face down using a damp cloth.

Cut two pieces of lining fabric to the same size. Cotton poplin or similar fabric would be suitable. Trim away the corners of all four pieces—not too close to the embroidery or it will fray.

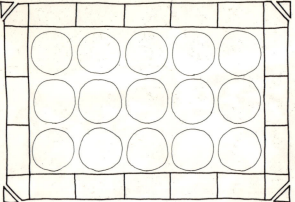

Turn in and tack down the edges of canvas on the sides and bottom, mitreing the corners neatly.

Press. Turn in eactly the same amount on the lining pieces, tack and press.

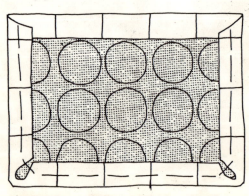

With right sides together carefully position a zipper of the length of the embroidered area over the embroidery. Taking the minimum seam on the zipper tape, tack together following the line of canvas threads to keep the edge straight.

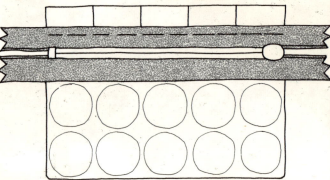

Tack one lining piece over the zipper, right sides of lining and embroidery together as shown below. Attach the other pieces to the opposite side of the zipper in the same way.

Turn so that the reverse side of the embroidery is facing. Machine or hand stitch the three layers together, taking the stitches actually into the last holes used for the embroidery and following the line carefully so that no canvas threads will show. Fasten off securely.

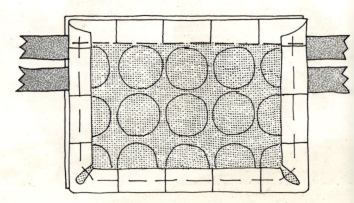

Open flat and press lining away from the inside of the zipper. Top stitch edges of lining pieces together. Fold embroidered canvas back over lining pocket and with matching wool oversew the edges sides and bottom together, tucking in the flaps of the zipper tape.

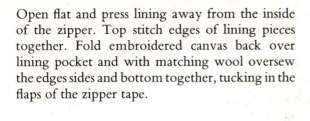

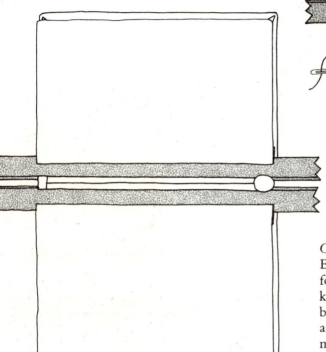

Overleaf
Everyone can find a use for a bright zipped case for keeping something safe—spectacles, pencils, keys and small change. Small pieces of embroidered canvas suitable for making these purses and cases could be worked by youngsters and then made up with a little help from an adult following the instructions given

A row of houses makes a good subject for an embroidery. Here the colours have been restricted to reds, giving unity to the design which has been kept as a flat pattern of windows and doors. A row of shopfronts with trees and railings and figures would make an interesting picture, or a more exotic silhouette might be remembered or copied from a photograph taken on a holiday abroad

Lettering

Try to incorporate lettering in some of the items to be made. Words and letters, initials perhaps, add to the decorativeness and interest of many designs.

Begin with one word—a child's name used on a pencil case or bag maybe. Space out the letters carefully, remembering that the pattern of spaces between the letters is as important as the letters themselves. Turn the design upside down and look at it to judge whether the spacing is correct. Use a piece of graph paper and work out exactly the size and spacing of the letters, before beginning the embroidery.

The name NANCY was made from letters taken from a Victorian pattern book of alphabets used for marking linen, and intended for cross stitch work of a much finer kind. Such an exercise could be framed and used to decorate the wall of a child's room. The names of all the members of the family worked in different kinds of lettering would make a good sampler.

Though elaborate letters are fun and look exotic, simple letters worked strictly to the angles of the warp and weft can be just as attractive if the tonal value of the letters and the background colours are carefully chosen. The illustration overleaf shows an alphabet sampler worked in the computerised letters seen today.

Overleaf
A twentieth-century sampler using computer type letters which lend themselves easily to the discipline of the canvas. Great enjoyment can be found in planning and arranging such pieces. Make a sampler using a name worked in many different kinds of letters using colour to unite them into a pleasing design

With the help of a sheet of graph paper many decorative letters can be devised which can be worked in embroidery. Collect interesting type faces or layouts and try to adapt them for making working designs inventing new letters when necessary to suit your purpose

75

Cotton furnishing fabric designed by Peter Perritt
Reproduced by courtesy of the Design Council

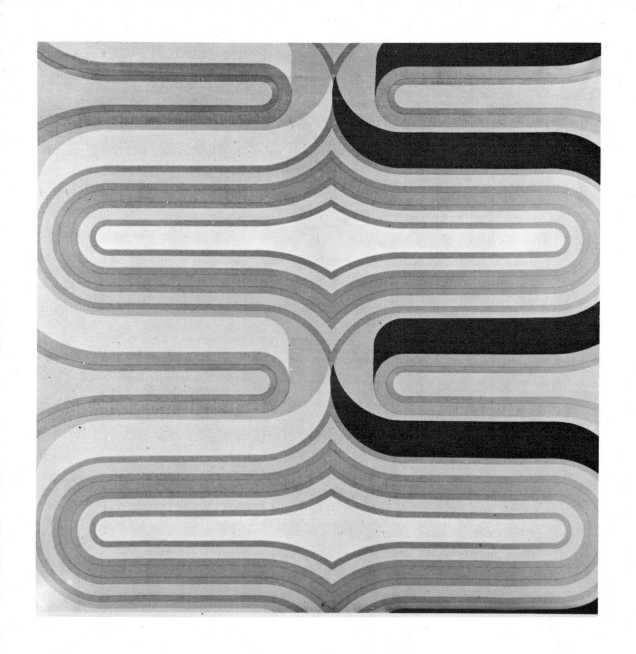

Cotton furnishing fabric designed by Peter Perritt
Reproduced by courtesy of the Design Council

Fashion accessories

A strip of embroidery can be the focal point of a hat. This can take the form of a band to trim a hat with a brim, and designed to complement an outfit. The fur patterns shown on pages 26 and 27 would be very effective used in this way.

A crown can be added to a worked band used as the basis for a hat. This could be of softly gathered velvet or wool jersey, brilliant felt or tweed. The contrast between the embroidery and other fabrics and textures makes for an interesting effect. A knitted or crocheted crown could also be made and attached to a strip of embroidery and finished off with a tassel, ponpon or trimming of plaited wools. Leather, now obtainable in many fashionable colours, or one of the new synthetic fabrics, would act as a foil for such a piece of embroidery and could be enriched with beads, buttons, or sequins.

For a young child an embroidered bonnet or coif is most attractive. In Elizabethan times the effectiveness of embroidery used in this way to draw attention to and frame the face can be seen in portraits of women and children of this period. Study the costumes of days gone by for ideas for the application of embroidery to dress, and see how cleverly it was used to show off any feature of dress or person. Sleeves and caps and stomachers, gloves, collars and cuffs were often richly ornate and the designs full of delightful detail that suggest a great enjoyment in the execution of the work.

◄ Embroidered bolero designed by the author. A bold floral design in pinks, blues and mauves on a lime green background makes a dramatic statement when worn with a plain dress. It would be equally attractive worn with a blouse and trousers, and a wide cummerbund
Reproduced by courtesy of Golden Hands

A small piece of embroidery made to be worn over a plain garment is an important addition to a wardrobe. It could be a bolero similar to the one shown on page 80 with floral panels, or a wide belt in bold geometric patterns.

A pair of beautifully worked cuffs that fit the wrists neatly can be worn with a plain dress or jersey. For the winter these could be lined or trimmed with fur, or quilted silk, and as well as being warm, would draw attention to pretty hands.

A child's walking reins or harness made of bright embroidery with straps buckled at the back and a row of jingling bells would keep a lively toddler amused and safe.

Slippers and light indoor shoes give plenty of scope for the use of embroidery and do not take long to work. A child's slippers or simple bootees would make a good first exercise in using embroidery for practical purposes.

For a boy or young man a 'rajah' collar and epaulettes embroidered in rich colours would give an air of distinction to a special party jacket, perhaps made in velvet. The weight of cloth must be taken into consideration when using canvas embroidery as a trim. It must not be used with flimsy materials. A band to be worn round the neck should be lined for comfort. For a straight upstanding collar some interfacing material should be used, the edges bound or trimmed with cord.

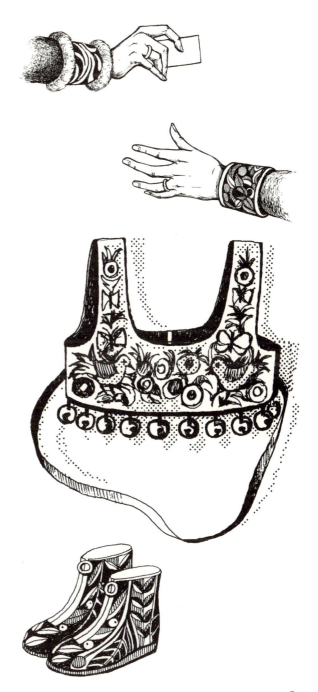

The addition of embroidered detail gives a new interest to any garment. Fringes of leather thonging swinging from a bolero for a youngster converts any outfit into one for dancing in.

Whenever items made from embroidery are to be worn they must be made up very carefully, preferably by hand, and the work lined and bound. A sewing machine can be used for joining pieces of canvas to the lining material, but always work at a very slow speed, keeping the seam close to the embroidered area. In most cases, as for the bolero shown, the lining and embroidery can be joined wrong sides together, right sides out, and the edges then trimmed and bound. Remember never to trim the canvas too close in case of weakening the embroidery.

Inspiration for design

No one aspect of learning is isolated from other kinds of knowledge. Getting to know more about any one thing inevitably leads to finding out new things about other related subjects. For instance, by making simple patterns for a chair seat, using the squared canvas, attention is drawn to similar patterns in one's environment.

Other people's solutions to the problem you are trying to solve can help to suggest new ideas. Textile and carpet designers have much the same problems as these media have some of the limitations facing the designer of canvas embroidery.

Plaits and chevrons and geometrical forms can be made to jump to life with the clever use of colour. The development of such structural designs which can give a *trompe d'oeil* effect will no doubt appeal to the more mathematically minded.

Pierced stucco window from the Great Mosque, Damascus

Pattern formed of overlapping octagons based on Spanish fifteenth century enamelled earthenware tiles in the Victoria and Albert Museum

Labyrinth from a Cretan coin. See also page 41

An old Victorian footstool is given a new look with an embroidered top worked from a design seen in an historical pattern book. It was adapted from a thirteenth-century inlay once in the pavement of the Cathedral of Amiens

Stained glass windows give an interpretation of natural forms in bold clear colours which adapt well to embroidery, even to the extent of utilisng the characteristic bold black outlines, which emphasise the brilliant reds, blues and greens.

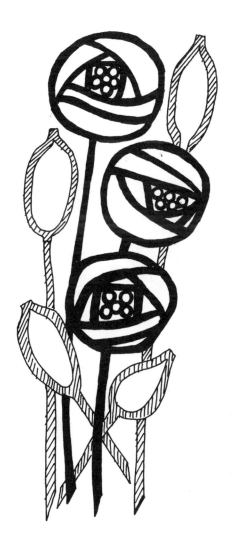

Detail of a stained glass window, Koenigsfelden, Switzerland

Design based on the wooden balcony rail from the old King's Head Inn, Southwark, London

Heraldry, flags and coats of arms offer dramatic colour play, and the bold symmetrical shapes are easily translated onto the canvas.

Wallpaper designed by Anthony Little ►
Reproduced by courtesy of the Design Council

Bow knot block pattern for weaving

Pattern on silk brocade, twelfth century,
Halberstadt cathedral

As one craft so often apes the characteristic patterns formed in another, fascinating designs can also be built up using weaving patterns. The criss-crossing of one colour over another gives a very rich and interesting mingling of colours, and enjoyment, in the planning and manipulation of the colour scheme.

The discipline of working within the warp and weave threads can lead to intricate and elaborate designs just as it does initially to simple geometric ones. Graph paper is a great help when working out more complicated ideas.

Many block prints, damask patterns and wall-paper designs are made as symmetrical shapes often using natural form or figures—which translate into embroidery very well—in a stylised way, using a central line and duplicating each side in a mirror-like fashion. In this case the squared canvas obviates the need for tedious counting and the design can be built up quickly and accurately as the work can be checked at a glance. This canvas also allows great scope in enlarging patterns to scale. A design worked from a central line does not need to be exactly the same on each side. For example, with a design for a figure the arm can be in different positions.

A visit to a museum takes on a new relevance if there are examples of work to see where other minds in other times have explored the possibilities of the craft. This embellishment of cloth by covering it with patterns and pictures worked with needle and thread has been a creative art form for centuries. Young people today might consider the designs on centuries-old canvas work to be the height of fashion.

Similar basic shapes for figures can be made into costume studies which give free rein to the decorative elaboration of historic costumes of all kinds.

For larger designs or panels, houses and architectural forms also adapt well to this method, so can any structure with regular positioning of arches, windows, or doors. Old samplers in which a formal suggestion of a house and its occupants was depicted are delightful, and such a record would make an entertaining exercise.

The façade of a house with some decorative lettering, the date and any other interesting details could become a treasured possession of future members of the family. An arcading of trees with figures between, members of a family or a group of friends, would make a wall decoration and be an original and pertinent way of commenting on their different characteristics.

Design from a Tudor house

Ideas from mediaeval manuscripts

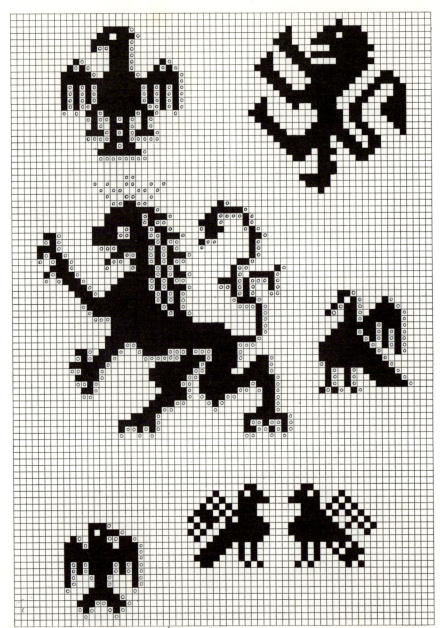

Rampant lions and heraldic birds from Victorian pattern book. These combined with lettering would make decorative commemorative panels for schools, clubs, etc.

We can see in the achievement of past generations this element in the human make-up—the need to express something about ourselves and our surroundings. Most beautiful and remarkable things have been achieved by using the materials that came to hand in an effort to achieve this. Any local museum bears the lively evidence of this.

There is a satisfaction in making something as well and as beautiful as possible and this gives to a commonplace article a quality that becomes a source of wonder and delight to following generations.

Though today we have many distractions in the form of ready made entertainment and diversion, we also have the same human impulse to satisfy, this need to stamp our personalities on the things we use and wear, and on our homes and surroundings. Mass produced items have a place but so have personalised ones. The most rewarding part of any creative work is the knowledge that it is unique.

I would like to think that this book will encourage more people to try to develop their own personal ideas and produce original designs.

For further reading and inspiration

Samplers, Donald King, V and A Museum Picture Book no. 14, HMSO

Order in Space, Keith Critchlow, Thames and Hudson

Bridget Riley, Maurice de Sausmarez, Studio Vista, London

Designs for Craftsmen, Walter Miles, Doubleday, New York; Bell, London

A Book of Signs, Rudolph Koch, Dover, NY

Pattern Design, Archibald H Christie, Dover, NY

Canvas Embroidery, Diana Springall, Batsford, London; Branford, Newton Centre, Mass.

Ideas for Canvas Work, Mary Rhodes, Batsford, London; Branford, Newton Centre, Mass.

The Technique of Woven Tapestry, Tadek Beutlich, Batsford, London; Watson-Guptill, New York

Small Woven Tapestries, Mary Rhodes, Batsford, London; Branford, Newton Centre, Mass.

A Treasury of Design for Artists and Craftsmen, Gregory Mirow, Dover, New York

Creative Drawing: Point and Line, Ernst Rottger, Batsford, London; Van Nostrand Reinhold, New York

Creative Paper Craft, Ernst Rottger, Batsford, London; Van Nostrand Reinhold, New York

The Observer's Book of Flags, I O Evans, Warne, London and New York

Japanese Emblems and Designs, Amstutz de Clivo Press, Zurich

Pattern and Embroidery, Anne Butler and David Green, Batsford, London; Branford, Newton Centre, Mass.

Inspiration for Embroidery, Constance Howard, Batsford, London; Branford, Newton Centre, Mass.

Design in Embroidery, Kathleen Whyte, Batsford, London; Branford, Newton Centre, Mass.

Samplers, Averil Colby, Batsford, London; Branford, Newton Centre, Mass.

Suppliers in Great Britain

Canvas, threads and embroidery accessories

Mrs Mary Allen
Turnditch, Derbyshire

E J Arnold
Butterley Street, Leeds

Art Needlework Industries Ltd
7 St Michael's Mansions
Ship Street, Oxford

Craftsman's Mark Limited
Broadlands, Shortheath
Farnham, Surrey

Dryad
Northgates, Leicester

Hugh Griffiths
Brookdale, Beckington
Bath, Somerset

Harrods Limited
Brompton Road
Knightsbridge, London SW1

T M Hunter
Sutherland Wool Mills
Brora, Sutherland

J Hyslop Bathgate and Company
Victoria Works, Galashiels

Mace and Nairn
89 Crane Street
Salisbury, Wiltshire

The Needlewoman Shop
146 Regent Street, London W1
also *squared canvas* and *graph paper*

Nottingham Handcraft Company
Melton Road
West Bridgford, Nottingham
also *squared canvas* and *graph paper*

Christine Riley
53 Barclay Street, Stonehaven
Kincardineshire AB3 2AR

Mrs Joan L Trickett
110 Marsden Road
Burnley, Lancashire

Suppliers in the USA

Appleton Brothers of London
West Main Road, Little Compton
Rhode Island 02837

American Crewel Studio
Box 553 Westfield
New Jersey 07091

American Thread Corporation
90 Park Avenue, New York

Bucky King Embroideries
Unlimited
121 South Drive
Pittsburgh, Pennsylvania 15238

The Needle's Point Studio
1626 Macon Street, McLean
Virginia 22101

Yarn Bazaar
Yarncrafts Limited
3146 M Street
North West Washington DC

Squared canvas and *graph paper*

Eric H Greene and Co.
11044 Weddington Street
PO Box 257
North Hollywood
California 91603

also obtainable through

S R Kertzer and Co. Limited
257 Adelaide Street West
Toronto 129, Ontario, Canada

Coats Patons (Australia) Limited
321–355 Ferntree Gully Road
PO Box 110, Mount Waverley
Victoria, Australia

William Brandt and Co. Limited
PO Box 1400
112 Lichfield Street
Christchurch, New Zealand

Raffles Agencies
45–48 Canada House
90 President Street
Johannesburg, South Africa